# Harnessing Motivation

# Harnessing Motivation

## 10 Steps to Overcoming Obstacles in Your Life

*By Denny Dey*

**Educational Management**
**P.O. Box 3478**
**Olathe, KS 66063-3478**
**EducationalManagement@worldnet.att.net**

Leathers Publishing Co.
4500 College Blvd. #310
Overland Park, KS 66211

Cover photo by Diana Oliver

ISBN 0-9646898-7-1

Library of Congress
Catalog Card Number: 97-070294

For Legal Care of Canada
memberships call
Mary Lou
519-291-3208

# Acknowledgements

I wish to thank the following people for their assistance in the course of this project: Ruth Dey, Del Dey, Jane Schaumburg, Ron Poplau, David Naster, John and Jayne Marsh, Mo Ediger, Diana Oliver, Gina Pope, Becky Gardner, Gary Forristal, Tim Quirk, James Brazeal, Wayne Ransom, and Tena Wood.

*This book is dedicated to
all who wish to
overcome obstacles in their lives
so that they might realize their dreams!*

# IS THIS BOOK FOR YOU?

Do you value motivation? Do you recognize motivation when you see or feel it? Do you know how to use motivation to get what you want and/or need? Are you willing to take time out of your busy lifestyle to learn more about motivation? Are you the type of individual who accepts and practices suggestions that, at first, seem contrary to your current ideas and beliefs?

The answers to these questions are important! If you value motivation and would like to know more about how to recognize and utilize motivation to get what you want and/or need, this book is for you!

If you are willing to take time out of your busy lifestyle to learn more about motivation, this book will share twenty-five years of observation, education, and experimentation with you!

If you are the type of individual who accepts and practices suggestions that, at first, seem unusual, this book will make a difference in your life!

This book is based on my highly successful seminar entitled HARNESSING MOTIVATION. I am going to share the approach that I have discovered on my twenty-five year journey along the path to success.

# HARNESSING MOTIVATION!

I started consulting when I was twenty-one years old. Since then, I have been a consultant to both education and business. I have motivated kids to use the library and teachers to use available resources. I have taught the business community to motivate themselves and I have promoted the value of motivation in the public arena, as well.

In the past twenty five years I have learned and now support this valuable realization:

## "Without motivation, I cannot make it happen!"

So, you may ask, what is <u>it</u>? It is whatever you <u>want</u> or <u>need</u> in your life. It is a personal quest that involves personal desires. It is important to <u>you</u>. It may or may not change <u>your</u> life. It may or may not be achieved. <u>But it is a primary focus in your life</u>! I promise to develop this idea more as we progress into the heart of HARNESSING MOTIVATION.

## "The greatest obstacle between you and success is you!"

# WHAT IS MOTIVATION?

Motivation is desire. Motivation is the "fuel" of action. Motivation is best represented in statements such as, "I can..." or "I will..." according to my experience.

Many people do not understand motivation. They believe that motivation comes from a cup of coffee or a cigarette. They are wrong! Cigarettes, coffee, candy, food, cars, toys, clothes, jewelry, and garage sales are not motivation. If you can put it in your mouth it is not motivation. If it has a price tag, it is not motivation. Motivation is not a reward. A reward appears at the end; hence, it does not exist now. Motivation is <u>now</u>. It is the fuel that gets us up and at "it"! Motivation propels!

## "Rewards are gifts that we select for ourselves. Motivation is the energy that creates action. Don't confuse the two!"

You can't live your life hopping from reward to reward. When you do this, you live for the product rather than the process. It is the process of living a motivated life that promotes fulfillment. Products are the end result of a fulfilling experience. When you travel toward a want or need you must pay attention to every step, every action, every experience in order to be fulfilled. Otherwise, you experience amnesia during the process phase and awareness only during the product (reward) phase. Such an approach destroys learning and continued achievement and creates frustration when rewards are not realized. Don't do this. It is a short term plan rather than a long-term relationship with motivation.

Let me begin this project with a story and then on the following pages I will share some of the same information that I offer in my seminar.

# THE PEDESTRIAN!

Last year, I travelled to a spot south of St. Louis from my home in Olathe, Kansas. On the way, I was grumbling to myself about how long it would take and how much I had to do and how wasteful the trip would be. I had a consulting assignment that would take three hours to accomplish and it irritated me that I would have to use thirteen hours of my time to get to and from the site.

Around noon, I jumped off the interstate and raced some papers to an office in the heart of Columbia, Missouri. I was skipping through town with no regard for anyone else but my-self, barely stopping at the stop signs, jumping on my accelerator at every opportunity.

I pulled up to a stop sign in the downtown area and, with-out thinking, went immediately to the accelerator after a good impression of a real stop. Luckily, out of the corner of my eye, I saw a woman in a wheelchair slowly rolling along the crosswalk.

I braked immediately and narrowly missed a catastro-phe. She looked at me and when she was satisfied that I meant her no harm she continued across the street.

# AMAZING!

What is most amazing about this occurrence is the fact that the woman was literally strapped into the wheelchair. The only method of locomotion for this woman was a joy stick placed upright on a flat board across the armrests in front of her head. She controlled the motion of the chair with her forehead! Her legs and arms were useless.

I made myself sit there and watch. I remember the feeling that came over me when she rolled along the sidewalk at the end of the crosswalk. I still remember the moment vividly.

(If you really understand the next statement, and I mean really understand what I am about to say to you, this book will be a great asset in your future plans. If not, I understand. Better luck next time.)

# A NEW PERSPECTIVE!

I encountered a new perspective on that day! During the morning, I had done nothing but complain and promote negative feelings about my situation and opportunities. Seconds after that incident I realized that I was lucky to have both mobility and maneuverability in my life. I had every reason to succeed and no reason to complain.

I watched this woman who had asked to be strapped into a wheelchair and allowed to control her own motion and I realized that my attitude deserved a severe reprimand.

"When you function in an unmotivated state, your attitude is a breeding ground for negativity!"

According to attitude: This woman, whoever she was, deserved to be a consultant with a fully functional body. I deserved a wheelchair!

# BIG DECISION!

I made a big decision! I decided on that day, that I would gather everything I knew about motivation during the past twenty-five years and I would deliver it to any and every "body" willing to read and risk!

"If you look for motivation you will find it everywhere you look!"

# SELF-SURVEY!

It was time for a self-survey! There is no job on earth that satisfies me more than motivating others toward their goal. I love to share ideas and avenues that lead to success. When I work with participants in the seminar, the time flies by. Everyone is learning and the energy is remarkable.

However, in the early 1980's I had a problem with the concept of motivating others. As an individual, my personal wants and needs were unique to me, alone. So, in my seminars I had difficulty adapting my motivational approaches to those of my audience. Also, I could find no single formula for motivation that qualified as a foundation for my presentations. Now what? Was I in the wrong business?

# RESEARCH!

I established a personal research plan. I reviewed stacks of reports, books, audio tapes, videos, and live presentations. I interviewed numerous people who used motivational products and services.

I spent time with people who were successful and people who were not. After years of observation and review, I determined that motivational offerings tend to come in the following recognizable formats:

1. EUPHORIC MOTIVATION presentations and products are designed to create a sense of well-being with no specific step-by-step plan of action. Examples include humor, storytelling, quotations, and some types of music. Presenters work with themes such as rags to riches, beating the odds, put on a happy face, don't give up, and faith in one's own abilities.

After dinner speeches are famous for displaying this type of motivation. Participants come away with a good feeling but very little content upon which they can design a plan of action for themselves. I know of organizations that think nothing of paying a famous person ten thousand dollars to speak for an hour after dinner. Euphoria can mean big bucks for the right speaker. But big bucks don't always provide effective motivation.

2. "MY WAY" SEMINARS and products promote a single plan of action as an effective route toward success that all may follow. An example is any live presentation or product that details the success of a single individual or group. Topics range from addiction to developing a successful business.

My book and audio tapes will most likely fall into this category simply because I mention ten steps to personal motivation. However, I tend to think of my work as a review of motivational processes and products more than a plan. MY WAY SEMINARS are developed after-the-fact by successful people with successful programs.

3. THE MULTI-STEP APPROACH utilizes a multitude of motivational styles and examples for the purpose of creating a wide range of "MY WAY" SEMINARS in one presentation. An example would involve the sharing of many different big names and accomplishments. MULTI-STEP is designed to offer you the most effective plan for any problem you encounter.

Topics are unlimited. Business and personal success are highly profitable themes. This approach tends to incorporate hard copy and audio tape along with an occasional video tape to cover a wide range of interests on the part of the buyer. Some people prefer audio tapes rather than books because they are short on time and commute each day.

THE MULTI-STEP APPROACH is perfect for the person who is trapped in an automobile on a daily basis. There are so many topics to choose from and so few hours to study in the life of the commuter. Audio tapes that echo popular publications find a welcome home in the automobile. Depending on the number of audio tapes involved, these motivational programs tend to be a little costly. But the public doesn't seem to mind.

## "Motivation is desired by many and understood by few!"

# WHERE DID I FIT IN?

I had been studying motivational approaches and formats with the hope that I would discover what you are, at this very moment, hoping to discover. I wanted footsteps painted on the floor along with easy-to-follow instructions so that I could join in and dance the dance of motivation! Where did I fit in?

I knew that I was capable of working hard to get what I wanted. I felt excitement in the face of a challenge. I thought that I had a positive attitude. But what I really wanted was a plan of action that would take these raw materials and forge some kind of *super-person* who could only succeed! Sound familiar?

I was frustrated beyond description. None of the approaches that I studied were overwhelming favorites in my search for a unique and promotional motivational plan. If a plan didn't work for me I could not represent it to the public. I needed to know that my ideas could be tested on a daily basis by the very person who conducted the seminar-ME!

# RELAX AND REACT!

For awhile, I gave up on the idea of motivation altogether. I turned down assignments and I lost my focus on the problem. Believe it or not, that may have been the best thing to do. Why? I needed to relax and react to my own motivational needs rather than the theories and practices capable of supporting my career.

I looked inside rather than outside and found answers that had earlier escaped me. I paid attention to my thoughts and the things in my life that I cared about.

In a way, I was learning to learn from myself. Naturally, I was unaware of what was happening. I had been so busy trying to come up with a magic formula for motivation that would support the lives of everyone in the world that I ignored my own needs.

Once I began to pay attention to me, I realized that my motivational level was not constant. I had motivated days when I was willing to tackle major problems and processes. I had un-motivated days when I wanted hang around the house and do nothing.

Likewise, I enjoyed some motivational resources more than others. For instance, I was more excited about listening to a speech than reading a book at that time in my life. I seldom started a day without music. I avoided people who were stuffy and self-centered.

These natural preferences were telling me something about my own needs and wants in the world of motivation. I found that my profile was very important to my work because earlier I had been attempting to teach pathways that were contrary to my own motivational routes.

Exercise: *During the next week, I challenge you to pay close attention to your natural motivational routes.*

*What do you do each and every day that qualifies as a motivational moment?*

*How do you attend to motivation in times of need?*

*Is there a preference that has been calling for your attention all along?*

# A NEW REALITY!

My self-survey taught me to look once again to the outside world of motivation. Only now, I had a personal preference to consider. I began to wonder if other people had personal preferences. Thinking about that possibility caused me to observe and interview real people with real opinions while, at the same time, reviewing countless motivational products and processes.

As a result, I realized that no single format mentioned earlier would work for me. No single product or presentation could accomplish everything that I needed to do for myself. No amount of EUPHORIA could overpower my insecurities.

No MY-WAY plan was diverse enough to meet my needs.  No MULTI-STEP approach invited me to dance along.

I realized that motivation was an ever-changing, multi-faceted source of energy for the "why" of my actions.  I realized that motivation was fuel that I could locate and use to help me achieve my wants and needs.

This was a startling realization!  I saw the world of motivation with different eyes.  I sensed the energy of motivation with renewed emotions!  I visualized success at the end of the path and I realized for the first time:

## "Every action I take will either delay or nourish success!"

# THE ACTION PATH!

With a new definition and appreciation for motivation in mind, I decided to create my own "ACTION PATH" using everything rather than something!

Exercise: *Look back on yesterday and recall your actions throughout the day.  Which actions will nourish success ("it")
and which actions will delay success?*

Nourish                          Delay

1.                               1.

2.                               2.

3.                                        3.

4.                                        4.

5.                                        5.

# TAKE ACTION!

People who are capable of achieving their wants or needs must take action! If you want a job, you must apply. If you want wealth, you must accumulate. If you need food, you must search.

## "In other words, action is first and outcome is second!"

Motivation is the driving force of action. It is the fuel that propels! Allow me to share a compliment I received after one of my seminars on HARNESSING MOTIVATION. I received a call from a participant who said,

## "Other motivational approaches have put fuel in my tank. Your seminar showed me how to find the gas station."

*To date, I have received no greater compliment.*

# I BELIEVE!

I believe that people must take action in order to achieve.

I believe that people must create an action path toward

their wants and needs.

I believe that, in order to sustain momentum, it is important to pull over to the side of the road and put needed fuel in the tank.

# INSTANT SUCCESS?

I also believe that people buy lottery tickets because they want a bolt of lightning to deliver their wants and needs without effort. I don't believe in instant success!

I was standing in line at a convenience store one morning. The customer at the counter was purchasing several lottery tickets. On either side of the customer were children who were in need of a bath and clutching candy bars (breakfast). I looked outside. The family vehicle was a running wreck. I was amazed that it would idle. The fenders were vibrating and there was a thick blue smoke cloud rising from the fractured tail pipe at the rear.

There were children in the car, as well. I know poverty. I understand how easy it is to fall behind in the human race. But, I was saddened by the fact that this person was bargaining the future of the family on a lottery ticket!

People who buy lottery tickets are trying to create instant success in their lives. They don't believe that their actions will promote success! I find this to be a very sad reality in our world. Earlier this year, I listened to a speaker talk about lottery winners. He said that most lottery winners end up broke because they have no prior experience with money management. On the other hand I know of individuals who made less than average salaries and still retired with financial security for the rest of their lives. Why?

## "For the price of one handful of lottery tickets you can purchase a book or audio tape that will help you improve your life and achieve your goals!"

I believe that my action path will lead me to my wants and needs!  Do you?

EXERCISE: *I challenge you to interview a successful person.*

*Ask the person to describe action taken on the pathway to success!*

*After the interview, compare the actions described with actions that you have taken, thus far.*

*Is there a difference?*

*Were you aware of this difference yesterday?*

# MY ACTION PATH!

A friend of mine told me a story about a high school kid who made thousands of dollars in one week with an idea that his father had earlier rejected as nonsense.

My dad told me a story about a man who walked several miles to and from a job that paid one dollar per day during the depression so that he could feed his family.

My wife and I had lunch with a man who once refurbished antique cars and now designs and builds resort hotels!

My brother-in-law survived cystic fibrosis!

A friend of mine once had a middle school student who wanted to become an astronaut. He did just that!

I know a single mom with three kids who completely turned her life around by training for a new career. The outcome was fantastic!

You may not know it, but there are, and always have been, people who create and travel an action path toward success! I have decided to do the same. How about you?

# TEN STEPS!

My action path must include the following steps in order to be a life-long journey toward success.

1.   *I must value motivation.*

2.   *I must realize that I possess inherent motivation.*

3.   *I must not accept gray areas in my action path.*

4. *I must understand the role of inherent motivation with respect to my wants and needs.*

5. *I must learn to focus motivation on my wants and needs.*

6. *I must seek to connect motivation and education in order to achieve my wants and needs.*

7. *I must identify and select ambient motivation.*

8. *I must harness ambient motivation to predict, promote and protect on the action path to achievement.*

9. *I must match the product/process with the challenge.*

10. *I must constantly use these beliefs to establish and maintain positive partnerships.*

Try to imagine how I felt when I realized that I could take actions each and every day that would eventually deliver success. I believed that if I were able to motivate myself on a <u>daily basis</u> I would eventually make "it" happen. I felt, for the first time, that I had control of the factors that would make me a successful person.

I began the seminars on motivation once again. But this time I promoted no single approach or plan. I presented the participants with numerous products and profiles and told them to select for themselves. I encouraged each individual to look inside as I had done. Then, I shared my own ACTION PATH as a model.

"Look inside with honest appraisal and realize that you can learn from you!"

# INSTINCTIVE BELIEF?

People were fascinated! Each participant realized that the world was rich in motivation. They realized that personal choice is a powerful motivator in itself! They re-affirmed an instinctive belief in the value of motivation. They could return to the demands of their lives with an <u>idea</u> or <u>product</u> that fit their scenarios and situations. Nobody walked away empty-handed!

At last, I had an honest and functional approach to motivation!

# STEP ONE!

## 1. I MUST VALUE MOTIVATION!

The first question I ask at my seminar is, "Do you <u>value</u> motivation?" If the vast majority of the hands in the room go up I know that these people are already on their way to utilizing the tools of the trade.

If only a few hands go up I know that I must spend careful and deliberate time promoting an appreciation of the <u>power</u> of motivation. One of the best ways to do this is to tell a story.

I tell the participants about a blind man who asked me to

teach him how to gesture when he was lecturing. I asked him why he worried about gestures when it was far more important to speak appropriately. He said that he knew how to talk but he had never used his hands. Apparently there is evidence to support the fact we see and mimic gestures at an early age.

This man had been blind since birth. He also said that he did not want his students to think he was inferior to the other teachers. When I asked him how he had come to this realization, he said that one of the criticisms he had suffered in his education classes (Believe it!) was "lack of gestures."

This man loved teaching. He loved kids. He loved history. He was right, though. He couldn't gesture to save his soul. In fact, when he tried to use his hands he looked like a fish flopping around the deck of a boat. My first reaction was to suggest that he keep his hands in his pockets and cut his losses.

Then, I remembered that he had a genuine passion for Civil War history. He especially loved to talk about Abraham Lincoln. I challenged him to deliver a lecture on the Civil War. He did. Ten minutes into the lecture I interrupted him with this question, *"Isn't it true that many historians consider Lincoln to be a dictator who avoided due process and coerced opponents to vote his bills into law?"*

I knew this blind man valued motivation because he was the kind of person who achieved regardless of his handicap. He had once put an entire radio kit together by feeling the parts with his hands while listening to his mother read the directions aloud. He had found his way to and from the university campus with no help, whatsoever. He had the courage to ask for help and he wanted to improve when others would have accepted their handicap and continued the status quo.

I was sure I knew how he would react to my question. At first, he tried to be diplomatic but I jabbed at Lincoln's reputation again and again until my friend had heard enough. After a lifetime of not using his hands to display emotion and assist the process of communication, this guy started defending Lincoln with a flurry of adjectives and reflexive motions that would bring any crowd to their feet. He looked like he was conducting Beethoven's 9th Symphony!

I tapped this man's inherent motivation because I knew it was there. It worked. He valued motivation, believe me!

# POWERFUL INGREDIENT!

I believe that people who do not value motivation are missing out on a powerful ingredient in the formula for success. When I enter a room I know that I am the most motivated person on-site. I must be motivated in order to achieve my goals. I am a motivator!

Therefore, I must be in a motivated state at the beginning of the seminar. If not, I fall prey to negative influences.

"It is important to get to your attitude before someone else does!"

# WHAT DO I HAVE TO DO TODAY?

I make a conscious effort to value motivation first thing in the morning. I do not allow my mind to drift away from thoughts about motivation. I never allow my mind to entertain thinking that centers on, "What do I <u>have</u> to do today?" I phrase my thinking by saying, "What do I <u>want</u> to do today?" Sometimes the answer is simply, "I want to make a difference!" That statement jump-starts my value system in the world of motivation because I know that if I want to make a difference I <u>will</u> make a difference.

Too many people get out of bed and start the day with negative introductions such as, "What do I have to do today?" The word "have" implies indentured service and emotional slavery. Or they say, "Oh no, it's Monday!" I once joked about "MONDAYITIS" at a seminar. I said that the issue is not Monday. The issue is action without motivation. I proposed that we allow America to stay home on Monday and go to work on Tuesday!

The four-day work week would cure everybody's ills! One of the participants raised a hand and said, "In two weeks everybody would be crying about Tuesday instead of Monday". I agreed! I laughed and offered up Wednesday as an alternative. Surely, a three-day week would make people happy about going to work. Within seconds everyone at the seminar agreed that even if a one day work week were legalized people would get up on Friday and moan, "Oh no! It's Friday!"

## "People who function without motivation are not functional!"

These people are not actively seeking out the value of motivation. They create a victim profile long before any action is initiated and they have impressed their positive thinking with a negative outcome! They become cheerleaders of doom! Day after day, they allow a preview of negative outcomes to lead them away from positive thinking.

After so long, they are helpless to alter a negative destiny. I have witnessed so many people who live lives that fall into this category. I can only imagine what might have happened if they had turned away from "have" and embraced "want" at the beginning of each day.

## "I possess the ability to focus my attention on whatever I choose!"

EXERCISE: *Begin tomorrow with the question, "What do I want to do today?" Continue asking this question every morning for one month.*

# STEP TWO!

## 2. I MUST REALIZE THAT I POSSESS INHERENT MOTIVATION!

I have a favorite exercise during the seminar that promotes the reality of <u>inherent motivation</u>.

I ask the participants to circle the number that best represents their motivational level on a scale of 1 to 10 with 1 representing the lowest and 10 representing the highest level of motivation.

Use the following diagram as a model.

LOW          MODERATE          HIGH

1    2    3    4    5    6    7    8    9    10

Then, I tell them this true story:

A young woman accepted her first collegiate head coaching position in women's basketball only to find out that public expectations for the season were less than encouraging. Moderate to average ability players and a lackluster recruitment program were no match for competition that bragged about outstanding talent and resources.

Women's games were played before the men's matches and crowd support was minimal, if at all. The media never mentioned her team as a contender for conference championship. In fact, a spot in the lower rankings was consistently predicted. After early losses and several key injuries, the season seemed hopeless.

But, the coach refused to entertain failure as an option. She doubled her efforts and increased her personal level of motivation. She reasoned, and rightfully so, that if her team did not accept success as an option, failure was eminent. She established a schedule in her personal life that allowed for greater review of her opponents strengths and weaknesses.

She constantly communicated a winning season to her

players and public. She spent countless hours reviewing options on the court for players who were healthy and willing to play. She took special interest in the healing process of injured players and encouraged them to push for a quick and healthy return.

She filled her waking hours with motivational plans and productive thinking and she turned her back on the idea of a mediocre season even though the public and the media had granted her that option.

The result was a championship season that sports the best record of achievement in the history of the program! Everyone was astonished! Everyone but the coach!

# CIRCLE THE NUMBER!

After telling this story, I ask the participants to once again circle the number that best corresponds with their level of motivation.

The results are always interesting. The majority of the participants note that their second number is higher on the scale than their first number. Why? I believe that the answer is inherent motivation. My experience leads me to believe that each of us possesses inherent motivation that, if nurtured and developed on a regular basis, is capable of exerting positive influence on achievement.

Are you familiar with the statement, "People are at their best when things are worst?" I believe that this statement is additional proof that each of us enters the world with inherent motivation. Properly developed, this internal mechanism can be a powerful ally.

So, isn't it interesting that my job is "to motivate" people to accomplish a goal? Well, let me share a professional secret with you. If the goal happens to be your goal, I do not need to motivate you. I need to help you tap your own inherent motivation. On the other hand, if the goal is not your goal, perhaps your employer's goal, I was not hired to motivate you. I was hired to convince you!

## "You possess inherent motivation!"

It is important that you realize this fact. If you nurture inherent motivation you propel yourself along the action path toward success. Inherent motivation is natural. It exists within each of us. I have spent twenty-five years watching inherent motivation present itself in the people around me. There is not doubt in my mind that I can count on you to excite and make use of your own inherent motivation.

LOW          MODERATE          HIGH

1    2    3    4    5    6    7    8    9    10

EXERCISE: *Select an entertaining or educational video that you consider motivational.*

*Before watching the presentation, mark your present level of motivation on the scale.*

*Make a second mark after watching the video.*

*Is there a difference?  Do you realize that you possess INHERENT motivation?*

## "There is a force in the universe.  It is called inherent motivation!"

# STEP THREE!

## 3.  I MUST NOT ACCEPT GRAY AREAS IN MY ACTION PATH!

I once heard a story about a man who got up every morning and went through the ritual of preparing for work with absolutely no variation in routine.  He drove the same route to and from the job and ate the same lunch each and every day.  He did only what he had to do to keep his job and never offered input to his superiors.

He accepted his salary without hesitation and he never sought advancement.  When he was not on the job, he was in front of the television.  He never travelled and he had no opinions regarding politics or religion.

His favorite word was, "whatever" and his favorite pastime was relaxation without commitment.  He never took classes and he did not care to learn more about his field.  He simply existed. He lived in a gray area. He had no dreams and he never allowed himself to be challenged.

To this day, I wonder how many opportunities and adventures passed him by.

# GRAY AREA?

There have been many moments over the course of my twenty-five year career when I have been in what I call the gray area of motivation. In other words, I was not motivated prior to, during, or after an action.

Note: I am not talking about nerves. Fear is a great motivator because it pushes your survival button. Effective as it may be, it can wear you down and leave you by the side of the road at a young age.

I am talking about the value of motivation at work. When I was in a gray area I did not think about why I should be motivated. I did not prepare myself for a particular event and I did not remedy a consequence with any type of motivation. I was functioning in a fog of un-motivated actions and reactions. I was existing rather than exerting!

As a result I was not capable of performing according to my potential simply because I did not bring my potential (inherent motivation) up to speed.

Also, I did not do my best work. I did not handle a situation as well as if I had been motivated. I did not take full advantage of all of the options for success. Many people function in the gray area.  Likewise, many people do not achieve, they simply exist.

I know from experience that when I function in a gray area:

1.     *I lose money on business decisions.*

2.     *I establish negative working relationships.*

3.     *I miss important opportunities to achieve.*

Ask yourself the same questions!  Have you lost money on a lame duck? Is it possible that you have a negative working relationship with a key individual?  Have you hesitated when you should have taken action toward achievement?

## "I have learned that any and all actions I perform in the course of my lifetime are or are not guided by motivation!"

I believe the same law applies to you!

Exercise: *Take the time to create a list of actions from your past that were not guided by motivation.*

*What was the outcome?*

*Would motivation have been a contributing factor in a more successful outcome?*

# STEP FOUR!

## 4. I MUST UNDERSTAND THE ROLE OF INHERENT MOTIVATION WITH RESPECT TO MY WANTS AND NEEDS.

To illustrate the role of inherent motivation with respect to wants and needs as well as its ability to remove the gray areas from the action path, I tell the seminar participants the story of my grandmother Dey who lived through two depressions.

After surviving the first depression alongside several hungry brothers and sisters and the second depression as a widow, she desired achievement. But she focused her motivation on the one thing that she had learned to value most: <u>needs</u>! She had spent much of her life without the basics that promote survival; hence, she always felt that life support was more important than toys. Consequently, she filled her life with needs rather than wants.

I used to marvel at the simplicity of her home and its decor. No frills. No unnecessary possessions. She worked hard and she was never poor again!

I focus on my needs such as food, water, and shelter in order to survive. Needs create a foundation for wants. Imagine what would happen if I transferred my level of intensity from the need category to the want category.

The best way to determine your potential for achievement is to imagine that someone is going to take away a need such as food, water, or shelter. How hard would you be willing to work to maintain the status quo?

The answer reveals your true potential as an achiever!

# POWERFUL FORCE!

When I ask this question in the seminar, everybody stirs with anticipation. Reality suddenly dictates a new set of rules for each individual. Everyone comes to the understanding that inherent motivation can be a powerful force if focused properly.

I am always amazed when I encounter this reality. I realize again and again that people possess a power that is significant and sure to produce results if properly nurtured and maintained.

Think about the world around you and determine for yourself whether successful people are able to define the difference between their wants and needs.

Exercise: *I want you to make a list of five wants and five needs. Think carefully about the difference between each item.*

*Wants*                          *Needs*

*1.*                             *1.*

*2.*                             *2.*

3.                              3.

4.                              4.

5.                              5.

*Now, look at your list and say it out loud to yourself.*

*I want...(*                                    *)*

*I want...(*                                    *)*

*I want...(*                                    *)*

*I want...(*                                    *)*

*I want...(*                                    *)*

*I need...(*                                    *)*

*I need...(*                                    *)*

*I need...(*                                    *)*

*I need...(*                                    *)*

*I need...(*                                    *)*

## "We do not know what we are capable of doing until after the job is done!"

# STEP FIVE!

## 5. I MUST LEARN TO FOCUS MOTIVATION ON MY WANTS AND NEEDS.

Look at the next diagram and notice that the word focus is in the middle of the triangle. On one corner is the word personal. Another corner is marked by the word professional and the third corner bears only a question mark.

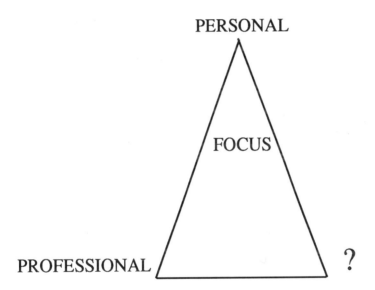

PERSONAL

FOCUS

PROFESSIONAL

?

## "Focus promotes intensity!"

This triangle represents our life focus:

We function professionally.

We function privately.

And, we spend as much time as possible attempting to figure

out the mysteries (?) of the universe around us.

# "Every person who reads this book or attends the seminar is involved in this triangle of focus!"

They have determined a need or want within the framework of their triangle and they seek the motivation to achieve. They have a goal in mind. Something has caught their attention and they are attempting to work it out, or work through it, or work toward it, or work around it. "It" is on the other side of a challenge that is fueled by motivation!

During the seminar, I look around the room as I speak and I see reactions and realizations that constantly reinforce this line of thinking. Every person in the room is there for a reason and that reason defines the triangle of focus.

I ask these people to share their focus with respect to the triangle and I hear numerous wonderful and insightful comments:

## Personal Focus
*"I want to become a better father and husband."*

## Personal Focus
*"I need to know that my family loves me."*

## Professional Focus
*"I want to get organized at work."*

## Professional Focus
*"I need to find a job"*

## ? Focus
*"I want peace of mind."*

## ? Focus
*"I need to know where I fit it?"*

To me, these comments reflect one or more areas of the triangle.

These people are paying attention to something (focus) and consequently put the "I want" or "I need" to work.

EXERCISE: *Look at your list of wants and needs!*

| *Personal* | *Professional* | *?* |
|---|---|---|
| *1.* | *1.* | *1.* |
| *2.* | *2.* | *2.* |
| *3.* | *3.* | *3.* |
| *4.* | *4.* | *4.* |
| *5.* | *5.* | *5.* |

*Now attach each item or statement to the appropriate corner of the focus triangle.*

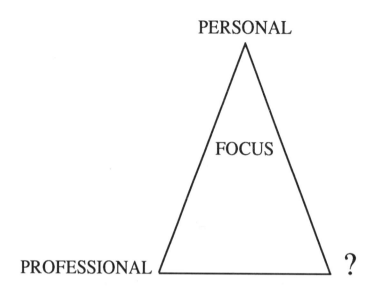

PERSONAL

FOCUS

PROFESSIONAL                               ?

"When you learn to focus motivation on your
<u>wants</u> with the same energy used to meet your
<u>needs,</u> you will achieve!"

# STEP SIX!

## 6. I MUST SEEK TO CONNECT MOTIVA-TION AND EDUCATION IN ORDER TO ACHIEVE MY WANTS AND NEEDS!

My problem is not one of creating motivation in people,
but one of constantly reinforcing the inherent motivation that
people possess. At the same time, I need to incorporate skill
building and information gathering to educate people about the
mechanics ( The process by which something is done or func-
tions.) of their wants and needs.

I had a friend who wanted to quit smoking. I knew that he possessed inherent motivation. I recommended a series of positive attitude tapes along with literature on health and fitness to keep him in a motivated state of mind; hence, he avoided the gray area and eventual doom.

In addition, the products and processes that I recommended included skill building and information gathering that approached the mechanics of tobacco addiction. My friend eventually used both the motivational and educational advantages of daily reading and listening behaviors to battle his addiction.

You see, if my friend was going to whip his addiction he would need more than motivation.

## "Goals are achieved with inherent motivation and inherited education!"

My friend needed to connect motivation and education. It was important to supply him with information about the mechanics of his focus: who, what, when, where, how, and why! These factors are important: He would need to know.....

* .....why he was so miserable without a cigarette!

* .....who to turn to for support and information.

* .....what the research on tobacco shared with the public.

* .....when he could expect his body to begin the process of functioning without nicotine.

*    .....where he could find resources designed to support his
     commitment each day.

*    .....how to live in a non-smoking environment.

# OPTIONS AND UNDERSTANDING!

Education is about options and understanding. Motivation is the fuel that drives us toward options and understanding. Education is the information necessary to succeed. Too many people shy away from the power of education. Fighting to get what you want with motivation and education is equivalent to using both hands in the prize ring. Using only one hand to defend yourself against negative influences is asking for a canvas sandwich!

I wanted my friend to succeed. That is why I incorporated education and motivation into his personal profile. He needed all the help he could get.

Another friend of mine simplifies the connection between motivation and education by saying,

## "I'm in the know and on the go!"

I believe that knowledge gained from both experience and study is vital to survival in the 1990's and beyond!

# PERSONAL EXPERIENCE!

I was involved in a car accident on May 16, 1980 that I

should not have survived.  If luck could be measured in dollars, I spent one million in one moment.  The end result was weeks of discomfort and physical limitations.

A friend of mine introduced me to bodybuilding and told me that I should study the mechanics of bodybuilding and start going to the gym.  At 149 pounds I truly looked like an accident victim when I entered the gym for the first time.

But, everyone was helpful and luckily there was an abundance of educational information (mechanics) available to me. The more I read, the more I was able to do.  I matched education and motivation to repair the damage and, as an added bonus, I eventually won a local bodybuilding title.  The title was not as important as the knowledge I had gained and the progress I had made in my understanding of motivation.

EXERCISE: *Think back on the last want or need that you pursued and ask yourself how you maintained daily motivation to achieve (...on the go!).*

*Also, ask yourself how much you knew (...in the know!) about the mechanics of the intended process or goal.*

# STEP SEVEN!

## 7. I MUST IDENTIFY AND SELECT AMBIENT MOTIVATION.

Ambient is an adjective that means "surrounding."  And it is.  There is an entire world of motivation at our disposal if we are in the frame of mind to seek it out and put it to use. Ambient motivation is literally anything and everything in my immediate frame of reference that might serve me. This realization changed my life overnight.

# VAST RESOURCE!

I suddenly felt as though I had a vast resource of input as an ally that would qualify my inherent motivation and educate me at the same time. Most of all, I liked the flexibility of my discovery. I have never been a "one plan man" when it comes to solving a problem or creating an avenue for success. I like flexibility and a mix of fundamentals. I am an idea guy. I don't believe that one tool is capable of fixing everything. To me, a tool is a solution to a problem. Multiple problems require multiple tools.

Ambient motivation was my cup of tea. I no longer had to fall back on a single success formula or paradigm of operation. Instead, I could reach into my bag of ambient motivation and select any and all that fit the profile of my goal.

# INFORMATION AND INSIGHT!

Where did I find ambient motivation? The first and most valued location is the public library. I found information and insight in abundance on the shelves of the very building I had driven by so many times. Thousands and thousands of books and tapes and records and videos and films on an endless range of topics served up more than enough motivation for my wants and needs Knowledge is power and the library is a power plant beyond compare.

I found ambient motivation in the bookstore! I located new and useful titles that dealt with time management, motivational programs, humor, lives of successful people, and innovative technology. All were quickly available to a hurried lifestyle.

I found ambient motivation in the record store. Music is highly motivational. I was attracted to a variety of titles and artists that fit a multitude of motivational wants and needs. My car doesn't run without the stereo!

I found ambient motivation on the television screen. I watch educational and motivational programs whenever and wherever I have the time. I consider my television to be a classroom!

## "Within the darkness there are many sources of light!"

I found ambient motivation in the video store. Current and past favorites serve up needed motivation on a regular basis. Call me emotional or sentimental, but I love a good movie that talks to the heart and offers hope rather than hurt!

I found ambient motivation outside my car window. I opened my eyes to the world: a truck driver battling the rain, a mother carefully picking up an injured child, two teenagers laughing uncontrollably on a park bench, an old man helping his life's companion into a wheelchair, a deer leaping effortlessly over a fence.

I found ambient motivation in the eyes and words of other people in the mall, supermarket, or elevator at a hotel. I began to realize how many people were searching for motivation in their lives. Their comments and insights were not only valuable to me but also inspirational.

I found ambient motivation in nature. Fishing on the edge of a quiet pond or watching the sun disappear beyond the horizon proved that nature has the key to motivation if one is ready to unlock one's eyes from the daily "heads down" struggle and look up.

Ambient motivation is anything and everything that serves to nurture and develop your inherent motivation. It is the fuel that propels. It is there for the taking. It is not prejudiced or particular and in many instances it is absolutely free.

Exercise: *Think for a few minutes about ambient motivation.*

*Remember that ambient motivation is any and all products and processes that serve to motivate and/or educate you along your individual action path. The choices that you make are totally up to you. The entire world is at your disposal if you know what to look for.*

*Locate and identify ten of these ambient motivations that exist in your world.*

*1.*

*2.*

3.

4.

5.

6.

7.

8.

9.

10.

*Think about products, processes, and people that you are drawn to in times of need, if necessary.*

# STEP EIGHT!

## 8. I MUST <u>HARNESS</u> AMBIENT <u>MOTIVATION</u> TO PREDICT, PROMOTE AND PROTECT ON THE ACTION PATH TOWARD ACHIEVEMENT!

So, how did I use ambient motivation in a way that nourished success? That's where the idea of harnessing (CONTROL THE ENERGY OF) ambient motivation takes over. I know that I am able to draft motivation from the world around me. I can achieve my goals with the help of great ideas, examples, people, and products. Whatever my focus, I can increase my odds for success if I am willing to harness ambient motivation.

EXAMPLE: I am impressed with the works of Robert Fulghum. His books are available in your library and neighborhood bookstore. One of his publications is entitled *All I Really Need to Know I Learned in Kindergarten.* My copy is published by Ballantine Books. Several short and inspirational chapters are available to my motivational needs. I read these chapters on occasion and I feel motivated as a result.

The thoughts shared by Fulghum are those that I might share with a friend in confidence. I find wisdom and comfort in reading them and their meaning translates to some task or mental state that will prove advantageous to me. Fulghum's work motivates and educates me toward achievement.

EXAMPLE: Beethoven. I find room in my motivational catalog for all of his music and, especially, the story of his life. His life was not easy and his torment was a source of public entertainment. His handicap was not as gripping as his talent. I like to use his music to focus my attention on a problem.

EXAMPLE: Carl Sagan. His efforts on behalf of our planet and his writings about current issues as well as the history of scientific investigation promote my desire to become a productive member of our time and world. I admire his achievements and I have used his techniques in several of my seminars. The *Cosmos* series is my favorite. He was, and always will be, a champion in my eyes.

EXAMPLE: I love working with school children. For twenty five years I have promoted reading in the schools via a motivational program called *The Storyteller.* The results have been outstanding. The students harness ambient motivation in their library and I harness ambient motivation in the students!

# COUNTLESS EXAMPLES!

Of the four examples listed above, I find it interesting that the first deals with a book, the second draws motivation from music, the third with the life and products of a prominent astronomer, and the final example draws energy from tens of thousands of children.

Obviously, I have countless examples of harnessing motivation in my life. Here is one of the most personal and powerful:

Some time ago I was having trouble communicating with my youngest son. In days gone by we were the best of friends and had a valued relationship. As he struggled through the teen-age years, our ability to communicate deteriorated to the point where both of us dreaded the next interaction.

Months before this conflict reached its peak, I had received a book from a workshop participant. The title was, *first you have to row a little boat* (lower case intended). My schedule was so hectic that I couldn't find time to read the Warner Book written by Richard Bode. I left it on my nightstand along with several others until it was covered with dust.

One night I could not go to sleep. I was in a painful self-appraisal regarding the situation with my son. I had tried everything to repair our relationship and I was unsuccessful.

My focus was my son. My want was to achieve success with him, once again. My need was love.

I noticed the book and decided to give my thoughts a rest. I opened it to the first page and began reading. What happened? If ever there was a clear-cut example of harnessing ambient motivation in my life, it is this: In Chapter Four, Bode describes "climbing the wind" in sailing. He talks about how sailors watch the jib to determine the point where the sail is climbing the wind without loss of momentum.

Loss of momentum? I suddenly realized that Bode was talking to me. I had lost momentum in my relationship with my son. My focus was personal and my desire was to guide my son along the path to success, as any father would expect. But, he was not complying. We were losing momentum. I had over-controlled the act of climbing the wind, sacrificing momentum in the relationship.

We were no longer growing together. We were growing apart. The next day I was motivated once again. I re-established contact with my son and watched the jib closely, so to speak. When the momentum of our conversation was jeopardized by fatherly advice and critical commentary, I backed off a bit and sought momentum rather than management!

The results were astounding. We talked for twenty minutes without friction. I discover, once again, why I liked and loved my son. I needed to know that we could still function together. To this day, I consider that moment(um) to be a major turning point in our relationship.

*I thank Richard Bode for his book and I hope that he does not mind my reference.*

# I SEE HANDS!

Whenever I illustrate methods of harnessing motivation during the seminars I see hands rise into the air above questioning expressions. When that happens I know that lights are beginning to come on all over the room. Connections are being made. Affirmations are developing!

EXAMPLES:

Q.     I like to listen to my favorite station on the way to work in the morning. Is that ambient motivation?

A.     It's that and more. You continually turn it on. You evaluate, select, and harness this ambient motivation every morning.

Q.     I play tapes of stand-up comedy in my car on the way home! Am I on the right track?

A.     Way to go! You're harnessing ambient motivation!

Q.     What is it when you read inspirational stories or novels at bedtime? I like to do that before I go to sleep.

A.     You are harnessing! When you read inspirational material at the end of a day you leave a positive impression of your achievements, as well.

Q.    I can't afford to take classes. Even with the money in hand, my kids need me at home. I have been self-teaching for awhile. I find "how-to" books and I study them after the kids are in bed. Does self-study qualify?

A.    I do the same thing! Ambient motivation is alive and living at your house!

Q.    So, the other day I'm in a flower shop to buy flowers for my wife. When I come out I'm excited about going home. Is it because I like flowers or my wife?

A.    (Everybody is laughing, now!) Probably both! But it is not uncommon for me to hear people cite the flower shop, pet store, the zoo, the museum, or ice cream parlor as ambient motivation. Purchasing the flowers is an example of harnessing ambient motivation! Did your wife like the flowers?

Q.    Is there a list of well-respected ambient motivations?

A.    The list is endless. I have some suggestions but it is important that you understand my philosophy of ambient motivation, first: The list that you discover for yourself is the one that you are after. It must be personal to be productive in your life.

Q.    Does ambient motivation always have to include an educational additive to be harnessed in order to be effective? What about music that doesn't teach a lesson or humor that simply relaxes me?

A.     No. Obviously, finding an ambient motivation that pos-
       sesses both motivation and mechanics would be a bo-
       nus, but not necessary.

       Believe it or not.  During the past five years, my semi-
nars and my life came together for the first time and I felt that I
had an idea I could stand behind!

EXERCISE: *List five scenarios where you have harnessed
ambient motivation during the past month!*

*1.*

*2.*

*3.*

*4.*

*5.*

# PREDICT-PROMOTE-PROTECT

       I learned about <u>predict-promote-protect</u> the hard way.
Remember earlier I said that my mental gray area was responsible for many of the negative actions and outcomes that over-
took me.  Allow me to share a story that illustrates the power
of predict-promote-protect as each applies to harnessing ambient motivation.

       I once taught in a high school located on the property of
a center for adjudicated adolescent males between 14 and 18
years of age.  These young men had committed crimes that

ranged from misdemeanor to violent offender. My job was to teach and their job was to serve their time and learn as much as possible before returning to society.

Many days I returned to my home full of despair because I knew that 70% of my students would not escape a prison term in their future. I was saddened at this reality and I felt helpless. What could I do?

I made up my mind that I was going to be the best teacher these young men ever had. I decided that, no matter what crime they had committed, I would be the most fair and positive influence in their lives. I demanded a positive attitude from myself and I worked as hard as humanly possible to maintain high standards as a teacher.

# PREDICT!

Every day I looked ahead to my schedule of students and classes and predicted the moments when I could make a difference (I want to make a difference.) at school.

I set my attitude up for success at those moments and I prepared my outlook (Harnessing Motivation) by reading biographies of influential people, listening to uplifting music, and studying teaching tactics that promoted learning in every environment.

# PROMOTE!

I promoted an image of a successful teacher. When the

moment came to present my attitude and ability I drew on what I had learned in my studies and never let go of the image of a successful teacher. I learned to live the role of an influential and informative adult in the heart of a prison atmosphere.

# PROTECT!

I did not allow my attitude and effort to be tarnished by negative output from students and staff. I avoided negative relationships and turned to my books, music, studies and hope.

# UNDER SCRUTINY!

I wish I could say that my efforts were totally successful. They were not. Many times I found my methods under scrutiny and eventually I was indirectly encouraged to resign due to continued unrest among those who saw me as a threat to the status-quo of the institution.

However, during the eleven months that I taught in lock-up and on-site I was never harmed by a student. In fact, many of the students told me that I was the best teacher they had ever had.

# THE HOOK!

Remember that people who function in the gray area are not on the action path.

* They do not value motivation.

* They do not realize that they possess inherent motivation.

* They do not understand the role of inherent motivation with respect to their wants and needs.

* They do not focus motivation on their wants and needs.

* They do not seek to connect motivation and education in order to achieve their wants and needs.

* They do not identify and select ambient motivation.

* They do not harness ambient motivation to predict, promote, and protect on the action path to achievement.

* They do not match the product/process with the challenge.

They sit on the hook of life and wait for the jaws of fate to swallow them alive!

I use predict-promote-protect every day of my life. I recommend that you do the same. At first, it may seem bothersome. Eventually, this approach pays big dividends.

EXERCISE: *Look at your triangle of focus and predict those moments when you must promote and protect your motivational level during the next 24 hours!*

*Make a list of ambient motivations that you might harness before, during, and after key interactions.*

# BEFORE!

| PERSONAL | PROFESSIONAL | ? |
|----------|--------------|---|
| 1. | 1. | 1. |
| 2. | 2. | 2. |
| 3. | 3. | 3. |
| 4. | 4. | 4. |
| 5. | 5. | 5. |

# DURING!

| PERSONAL | PROFESSIONAL | ? |
|----------|--------------|---|
| 1. | 1. | 1. |
| 2. | 2. | 2. |
| 3. | 3. | 3. |
| 4. | 4. | 4. |
| 5. | 5. | 5. |

# AFTER!

| PERSONAL | PROFESSIONAL | ? |
|----------|--------------|---|
| 1. | 1. | 1. |

| 2. | 2. | 2. |
| 3. | 3. | 3. |
| 4. | 4. | 4. |
| 5. | 5. | 5. |

"Motivation is your ally in the days ahead. It is a process that promotes achievement. It is a product that prepares you for the challenge!"

# STEP NINE!

## 9. I MUST MATCH THE PRODUCT/ PROCESS TO THE CHALLENGE.

I repeat the above several times in my seminar because it is important. I then drive home the following point:

*Match the product/process or (ambient motivation) to the challenge (focus) to predict-promote-protect both you and your chances for achievement.*

This is the key to staying on your action path. When you are on the action path you are harnessing ambient motivation with the intent to predict, promote, or protect. You value motivation that is both inherent and ambient and you are getting into a motivated state of "I can...I will...I am...I do!"

You have focused on one corner of the triangle and you

are now going to match the product/process (received via ambient motivation) to a challenge (How to get what you want or need.)

Here are some ways that I match the product/process to the challenge.

PROFESSIONAL EXAMPLE: When I have a seminar or meeting scheduled I select an ambient motivation such as a passage from a book or poem (product) or perhaps a list of do's and don'ts (process) to review before the event.

My challenge is that I must be mentally prepared prior to beginning the seminar. Therefore, I select ambient motivation that creates the desired response before I begin working with others.

PERSONAL EXAMPLE: Before returning home to my wife I play music (product) that is special to our marriage and I commit my thoughts (process) to the positive memories of our relationship.

My challenge is that I have my work on my mind rather than concentrating on my marriage. This is not fair to my wife. I select ambient motivation that has little to do with work and a direct relationship to my marriage!

? EXAMPLE: I like to spend time by myself after a particularly difficult assignment.

My challenge is that I must review my work with respect to my wants and needs. I can't allow outside negative interferences to inhibit my performance or self-evaluation. During those times, I open my books (product) on religion, science, philosophy, and history. Specific music helps me focus my attention. Nature (process) also helps.

# BIG DIFFERENCE!

There is a big difference between the me that arrives on the scene in a motivated state of mind and the me that arrives on the scene in a gray area. Without a chance to predict-promote-protect, I know that I decrease my chances for achieving my wants and needs.

## "Matching the product/process with the challenge offers options that I would rather not live without!"

During one of the seminars, I had just finished talking about predict-promote-protect when a lady raised her hand. She said that she had suddenly realized why her teenager roared into the school parking lot with the car stereo blasting out into space every morning! I knew instantly that the teenager was harnessing ambient motivation. School challenged the teenager! Music was an ally!

If you look around you will find people who are unknowingly harnessing ambient motivation. It is a natural and productive activity. I did not invent this tactic. I experienced it!

EXERCISE: *Select a challenge that you must attend to during the next week!*

*With respect for your wants and needs, select an ambient motivation that will nourish a positive outcome.*

*Answer:*

# STEP 10!

## 10. I MUST CONSTANTLY USE THESE BELIEFS TO ESTABLISH AND MAINTAIN POSITIVE PARTNERSHIPS.

Look at the diagram of the battery on the next page. Positive energy flows from person to person and person to process much like the battery in your car.

* The positive pole is the source of energy that runs your headlights so that you can proceed in the dark of night.

* The negative pole connects to the frame of your car.

* The path of electricity is from the positive pole to the lights.

* A connection is made between the lights and the frame of the car so that the circuit can be completed.

We function the same way in our relationship with the people and processes around us. We send energy out and we hope the circuit is completed.

```
        +                                      -
Positive Pole * * * * * * * * * * *Negative Pole
*                                              *
*                    BATTERY                   *
*              (INHERENT MOTIVATION)           *
*                                              *
Lights * * * * * * * * * * * * * * * * * * Frame
```

But, if we send energy out and receive little or no energy in return, we run out of juice, so to speak. The metaphor of the battery is important to you and me. We need positive energy in our batteries in the form of motivation. If someone or something is draining our motivation we will not be able to see our way.

I know many people who have <u>positive</u> <u>partnerships</u> established with the world of ambient motivation. All of these people are harnessing on a regular basis; hence, they have developed positive partnerships that align with their wants and needs.

These partnerships serve to promote and protect their motivational level and guide them along their action path from challenge to challenge.

My books, audio tapes, videos, music, friends, and family are ambient motivations. I have chosen these motivations as positive partners because I know that I am better able to succeed if I do not stand alone.

EXERCISE: *Look at the diagram below.*

*List five positive partnerships available to you under each ambient motivation.*

*These are the targets that you will harness.*

*Think about your goals as you select each ambient motivation.*

*Be realistic!*

# POSITIVE PARTNERSHIPS

| NATURE | LITERATURE | MUSIC |
|--------|-----------|-------|
| 1. | 1. | 1. |
| 2. | 2. | 2. |
| 3. | 3. | 3. |
| 4. | 4. | 4. |
| 5. | 5. | 5. |

| PEOPLE | AUDIO TAPES | HEALTH |
|--------|-------------|--------|
| 1. | 1. | 1. |
| 2. | 2. | 2. |
| 3. | 3. | 3. |
| 4. | 4. | 4. |
| 5. | 5. | 5. |

Note: This exercise *is best accomplished on the move. Keep your eyes and ears open to the world of ambient motivation. Remember, it is everywhere. If you are looking, you will find more than enough. Consider it a research project that takes place at the library, bookstore, record store, etc.*

"What price are you willing to pay......for a dream come true?"

"How hard are you willing to work......to achieve your goals? "

"How long are you willing to hold on......to your desire and dedication?"

I have asked myself the above listed questions more times than I can remember over the past twenty-five years. The answers are always motivational!

# MOTIVATIONAL PLANS FAIL?

My experience leads me to believe that our motivational plans fail for the following reasons:

1.  <u>We set goals in our "euphoric" state and when the glow wears off we have no interest in grinding out an effective plan of achievement</u>. Too often, I have witnessed individuals who commit themselves to a motivation only to return to their "old ways" as soon as the initial thrust of energy begins to fade away. This happens in addiction programs and weight loss plans as well as study habits and performance goals.

How does harnessing ambient motivation help? A little at a time. I consider harnessing to be the equivalent of a time-release capsule. Harnessing works with your motivations each day.

When you consistently select and use an ambient motivation you are in a position to be reminded of your wants and needs more often. You gradually gather information that suggests daily actions toward your wants and needs.

Each experience provides support for each step along your action path. You might read a chapter from a book, listen to a specific audio tape, enjoy specific selections of music, or converse with a mentor on a daily basis. All of these examples, and more, provide momentum.

2. <u>We are better trained at failure than success</u>. Our history of failure and lack of training in successful goal achievement covers many facets of our lives. The reality of achievement is that failure is not only the first step to success but often the stairway to success.

We are not able to maintain a plan or set of plans capable of protecting our motivation during a series of failures. Soon, we drop back to our former habits and behaviors. After awhile we begin looking for the failure profile long before we reach our intended goal.

How does harnessing ambient motivation help? Harnessing allows us to taste success in smaller portions on a consistent basis. Daily doses of positive input and motivational reinforcement gradually condition us to accept success as a real possibility.

The more we read about success, the more realistic it becomes. Modeling the lives and habits of successful people helps us to make effective decisions. Reviewing proven formulas for success helps us align our actions with winning ideas.

3. <u>We have an unrealistic perception of time and effort and their relationship to achievement</u>. We set goals that create a sense of "I can" and then realize that we must continually maintain this level of motivation over an extended period in the face of previously unknown adversity. The road is long and hard, so to speak.

How does harnessing ambient motivation help? Others have taken daily steps toward their successful achievement of goals. Harnessing their energy and studying the depth of their effort helps us to realize that the reality of hard work need not be a deterring factor.

Many successful people are students of success. They have spent valuable time reviewing the process of time management, organization, communication, finance, human resources, technology, and much more. They understand work ethic because they know that work is essential to success.

4. <u>The people that we associate with do not share our goals and motivations</u>. This is evident in the number of divorce actions that occur each year. It is also evident in the profile of work place conflicts. "I can" and "we will" are not always compatible.

Often times, friends will go into business together and soon find that their friendship is destroyed due to this problem. More than once, a participant has shared a story that proves this fact to be true.

How does harnessing ambient motivation help? Harnessing allows us to maintain a relationship with our loved ones or work companions while at the same time developing a relationship with positive products, people, and processes outside our immediate circle of associates. Ambient motivations are readily available as positive partners on the action path to success.

> "There are many reasons for failure.
> There are many ways to fail.
> Your chances of failure are great.
> So what?"

5. <u>Our goals sometimes change before we reach a state of accomplishment</u>. This is appropriate to business and industry, especially when the customer makes constant demands on the product or service. Sometimes, in our effort to catch up, we find ourselves on the way, but never there.

How does harnessing ambient motivation help? Harnessing incorporates a multitude of varied and viable formats. The ever-changing reality of variety in harnessing ambient motivation stands ready to accommodate a shift in assignment. It makes sense to be flexible these days.

There is no limit to the number of ambient motivations

in this world. Variety is your best friend in the last decade of this century.

6. <u>We get caught up in the trap of 50/50!  We believe that if we don't achieve the goal as it is stated we have failed.</u>  Right or wrong, in or out, up or down, left or right and other comparisons lead us to the 50/50 plan.  In my seminar I drive this point home with an exercise that pretends to have one right answer.

If participants get the right answer they have achieved their goal.  A wrong answer equals failure.  Then I explain that this is propaganda because 50/50 isn't realistic.  When we achieve a goal or do not achieve a goal there is room for both achievement and failure.

How does harnessing ambient motivation  help?  Harnessing provides us with countless examples of others who have struggled and survived.  There are no realistic examples of perfection.  Trial and error is a common theme in the profile of a successful life.

7. <u>Sad as it may seem, some of us want to fail because we get more attention for failure</u>.  We have become addicted to pity and remorse.  We realize that others will listen to our problems and we find ample reinforcement for failure in popular music or T.V.!

How does harnessing ambient motivation help?  Harnessing can create a new way of thinking about the "why" of our actions.  As we harness, we review a variety of plans and products that ask us to question our motives and create new resolutions.

The key word is reinforcement. If we, as humans, can be reinforced for negative behavior, it would seem feasible that we are capable of seeking reinforcement for positive behavior. Ambient motivation provides plenty of examples of positive behavior and its rewards.

8. Success scares us because we associate increased responsibility with success and fear that we cannot handle the additional load. In a way, we see success as the pathway to failure.

How does harnessing motivation help? Harnessing involves every imaginable resource in your bookstore or library. There are countless topics available to those who wish to deal with increased responsibility. Others have felt the pressure of success. What did they do, as a result, to increase the quality of their lives?

9. When goals are not achieved, people tend to change environment rather than behavior. I once had a boss who told me that he would call for references on new applicants to determine why they had left former employers to work for him. Invariably, he would find out that these applicants left a situation where they could not get along with others, perform according to original agreements, act responsibly, etc. He said that people tend to change places rather than faces.

I now know what he meant. I know of many people who take their inability with them on the road to find success in some other back yard. They haven't learned to make internal changes that promote success. They seek external answers to the internal wiring diagram for failure.

How does harnessing ambient motivation help? Harnessing motivation allows the traveller to learn on the road. People change slowly, if at all. Bad habits that denote achievement gradually weaken under the scrutiny of constant review, provided that enough examples are allowed to surface.

Reading and listening and studying about successful formulas and functional people gradually educates the wanderer to "look homeward, angel".

10. People are successful. But, they displace their motivation on wants and needs that are meaningless in the long-term relationship with fulfillment and responsible living. We see, we want, we charge, we use, we go on! The world is full of immediate gratification and instant answers to unscratchable itches.

People are enabled by their credit cards (which I don't accept) and their credit rating and so they believe that they can get whatever they want. They set their sights on meaningless items and displace valuable motivation with daily purchases and processes that enslave them to the very thing that they are escaping: indentured service to their debt structure and low motivation profiles supported by substandard wages.

How does harnessing ambient motivation help? When we surround ourselves with motivational products and services we grab onto the lives and learnings of people that we eventually admire and want to model our lives after.

We hear information from agreeable sources that tell us to put our toys away and apply our abilities in positive actions that will benefit our tomorrow rather than our today. We learn to build character as we build our future.

## "Do something for your future every single day!"

EXERCISE: *Look at the ten reasons for delayed success and prioritize them according to your life.*

*Which reason is most influential in your lack of achievement? Place that number at the top of your list.*

*Work through the list until the least influential reason for failure is at the bottom of your list.*

*If you could eliminate one of these reasons from your achievement profile, which one would it be?*

1.

2.

3.

4.

5.

6.

7.

8.

9.

10.

*Look back through this book and select a strategy to combat the negative influence you have selected.*

## "Your willingness to learn is the single most influential factor in the successful application of inherent motivation!"

# FAILURE EQUALS EDUCATION!

Each of the above problems is realistic. Every day I find myself facing one or more of the above realities in my own action plan. When I set goals for myself and hope to achieve them by harnessing ambient motivation, I instantly acquaint myself with the probability for failure.

Too many people fear failure. They believe that failure is the end. I disagree. I see failure as a beginning. Failure is my best friend on the way to success because it teaches me what to look out for! When the patterns return I am ready for them.

I attempted to coach a competitive sport only once in my life. Experienced coaches warned me about the pitfalls but

I would not listen. I wanted to motivate! I coached for one season and never won a game. I lost the respect of my players, my fans, and my boss. I was fired and I left the job ashamed. But, I did not let the failures I had experienced dissolve my chances for future success.

Instead, I analyzed what I had done and paid close attention to the value of each mistake. I then set my goals for the upcoming year and proceeded to have the most successful <u>financial</u> year of my life!

I have been married three times. My first two marriages ended in disaster! No matter how successful I was professionally, privately I was in pain. After the second marriage fell apart, I thought seriously about giving up on marriage, altogether. But I did not want to become bitter and hateful like so many others who have experienced failure in a relationship.

I decided to review my role in both marriages and I looked for mistakes rather than blame. I sought outside motivation and education and I looked toward the future with hope rather than remorse. The result is a marriage that borders on perfect with a woman who is my best friend and most prized acquaintance!

I lost a ton of money on a bad business deal years ago. I lost my car, my possessions, my credit, my creditors and my hope for immediate repair. I drove a twenty-five dollar car and ate spaghetti six times a week. I slept on the floor and painted my lawyer's house to reduce my debt structure.

But, I did not give up! I reviewed the reasons for my fail-

ure and I formulated a plan that drafted motivation and education on a daily basis.  I took classes and made new contacts
and constantly reminded myself that the only way to go was
up.  And I did!

EXERCISE:  *Look back on a similar failure in your life.*

*List the knowledge you have gained as a result.*

*Knowledge:*

*List ten ambient motivations capable of sustaining that
knowledge.*

*1.*

*2.*

*3.*

*4.*

*5.*

*6.*

*7.*

*8.*

*9.*

*10.*

*Set a date to gather one or more of these ambient motivations for future use.*

*Mark the date in your calendar and don't miss the appointment. It is a big day!*

# SOMETIMES!

Sometimes, before an important seminar or speaking engagement, I sit by myself for a moment and think about the hard work, hard times, and hard choices in my past. I realize, at that moment, motivation is a powerful ally. During a seminar, I don't hear my name when it is called because I know that my name is not what is important. I don't hear the applause that follows my introduction because I know that I haven't earned it, yet. Instead, I hear a voice that says, "It's time to go to work!"

## "There is a powerful motivational relationship with past failure and future success!"

# WHAT DOES HARNESSING MOTIVATION SOUND LIKE?

The following statements are taken from actual conversations I have had with individuals who harness ambient motivation.

**"I know what to do!"** This statement is indicative of individuals who take the time to learn as much as possible with regard to past failures and future success. These individuals learn to live in a state of motivation that produces the results required for success. They use <u>education</u> as a tool to achieve. They consider learning to be an ability that is appreciated and applied by those who respect knowledge and its power. When they open their ears and eyes to knowledge, they harness ambient motivation!

**"I can handle it!"** No matter the outcome of a particular action, these individuals possess sound self-esteem. They base their attitude on prior <u>experience</u>. They know that prior experience is valuable and they feel they are capable of making the right decision, when necessary. These people seek both knowledge and experience as powerful allies. They harness ambient motivation from the world around them and store the results of their daily efforts in their memory and regard those memories with pride.

**"Give me another chance!"** These people are highly appreciative of education, experience, and <u>effort</u>. They know that failure is predictable but failure to continue is pitiful. They are not frightened of failure during a first attempt because they know that many who have succeeded did so on the foundation of prior failures. They want another chance because they are capable of success more than failure and all that they desire is a chance to prove themselves. They harness the ambient motivation of <u>education</u>, <u>experience</u>, and <u>effort</u>!

**"No problem!"** These individuals are thankful for the chance to apply education, re-call experience, promote effort, and <u>envision</u> opportunity for success rather than options for failure. These individuals are capable of turning their attention toward possible solutions; hence, they harness ambient motivation and the power of positive thinking, prior achievement, and professional input to make "it" happen.

# THE SEMINAR

Perhaps the most productive aspect of the seminar is the variety of products and publications brought to the site. Harnessing ambient motivation depends on numerous inspirational and functional books, videos, audio tapes, and interactions available at the seminar.

People come to the seminar hoping to find a "step-by-step" approach to motivation and end up finding that the entire world is a motivational resource. They select books that fit their needs and wants and they use the audio and visual resources that reinforce their particular lifestyle and learning style.

I am relieved when I see participants share ideas they have gathered from a publication or product. I sometimes watch their faces as they review the literature and smile along with them when I know that they have found something that they can relate to easily.

I get a good feeling when I see participants walk out of

the seminar with products that will serve to motivate them along their action path.

The same applies to you, as you read this book. Maybe it is not possible for you to attend or schedule a seminar. But, the ideas in this book are for you, nonetheless. If you are on the starting line of your action path you are taking the first step toward a goal or achievement.

Don't go alone! Use the bookstore or library or record store or local zoo, if necessary. But, don't go alone! Ambient motivation is everywhere. Tap it's many resources.

# POWER STATEMENTS!

Get ready for some of what I call my "power statements" during the seminar. These are usually quite provocative and prone to emotional delivery!

# THE POWER OF PERSONAL SELECTION!

I believe that harnessing ambient motivation is an important first step for so many who wish to achieve "it" in their lives. Hopefully, by now, you realize that I am sincere when I share this belief with you. I also believe that there is no greater power on earth that can make a difference for you than the one that you choose for yourself. If you desire to achieve and have begun the first steps along your action path, I commend you.

But, if you have already found a motivation and begun

the process of harnessing, I applaud you!  Why?  Because I know that the choice is yours and the outcome is going to be yours, as well.  You make the decisions that drive you toward your goals, your wants and needs.  You now possess a powerful weapon against lethargy and failure because it is your weapon of choice.  The power of personal selection (harnessing ambient motivation) is incredibly potent in the future of your success.

When you find a book, or person, or theory, or song, or poem, or movie that fuels you forward toward achievement you have found the key to consistent and measurable improvement!

# ADVANTAGE VS. ATTITUDE!

I once read that attitude is everything!  I agree up to a point.  Without attitude on your side your chances of success are reduced.  However, I believe that it is possible to have a great attitude and never get what you want or need in life.

I personally believe that advantage is everything!  Harnessing ambient motivation allows an attitude to get an advantage.  With resources and resourceful people on your team you are better able to use education and experience to endeavor toward and envision future success.  In a contest where advantage versus attitude, put your money on advantage!

When you harness ambient motivation, you have a distinct advantage.  Never stand alone when you can stand as one among many who share a common goal.  Through the power of personal selection you have the ability to collect forces that share your goals and assist you in the days ahead.

I consider the ambient motivation in my life to be my closest ally when I am facing a challenge. I know that I am working with products and processes that will promote me. I have no fear of failure. I know that I am not alone.

# CONFLICT IS A PERCEPTION?

I believe that conflict is a perception. People who find themselves in a conflict over resources and power must first perceive that a conflict is taking place. The more I learn about harnessing ambient motivation with respect to its many resources and information the less I perceive conflict in my world.

I have begun to see what I used to call conflict as a proving ground for the vast number of ambient motivations around me. I used to dread conflict because along with my perception of its existence came a natural fear of failure to overcome its effects. Now I see the same situations in a new light. I think about what I have learned and what I can learn rather than what I have lost and will lose. Interesting, isn't it?

# UNDER PRESSURE!

Managers, law enforcement officers, physicians, teachers, lawyers, judges, politicians, mothers and fathers and so many others find themselves under pressure to have all the answers and never make mistakes.

I believe this is the road to ruin. Nobody is perfect and everybody makes mistakes. Yet, so many have problems living happily under realistic conditions when unrealistic expectations promote perfection as a model.

Harnessing ambient motivation helps people under pressure to find answers and ally with resources and resourceful people in the face of un-realistic expectations. "No man is an island entire of itself!"

# DIRECTED LIVES!

Too many people live directed lives! They have very little control over the direction of their lives and they are trapped in the mechanics of simply existing. I find this reality disturbing.

I choose to do what I do, regardless of the fear of failure, because I want direction rather than to be directed. I want to work for myself. I want to take risks. I want to make "it" happen.

I do not want to be a slave to someone else's wants and needs. That reality is not an option for me. I have worked for others in the past and it wasn't good for me.

I need to challenge myself every single day in order to be happy. In short, I have the desire to achieve and I harness ambient motivation to insure that I live a life that has direction rather than one that is directed by others who do not share my wants and needs!

How about you?

# YOU AS A MODEL!

Do you realize that your family, your friends, your associates and those people who encounter you for the first time see you as a model of something? This is true. Each of us is a model of something in the eyes of the world around us. Our whole society is based on models of stereotypical categories such as woman, man, rich, poor, old, young, happy, sad and thousands of other descriptors.

Think about the fact that you can become a model of motivation to those around you. It is more than a possibility. It is a reality. If you are not motivated you will never be able to model the virtues of motivation. If you harness ambient motivation and spend time working with it on a daily basis, others will witness and respond to your new category.

I have suggested that parents spend one hour per week sharing ambient motivation with their children. Take time out to seek and compare motivations with your loved ones for one month and determine for yourself if this action is beneficial. I say it is!

# NATION OF LEARNERS!

I have scouted hundreds of school systems in this country without finding a single curriculum that devotes a class to the theory and application of personal motivation. Why?

When I have presented my seminar in high schools and

middle schools I have witnessed exuberance and enthusiasm. How is it that we can demand so much motivation from a nation of learners without formal instruction and research into the world of ambient motivation?

# PERSONAL MOTIVATIONS!

If you want to learn about the personal motivations of the people around you take a look at the ambient motivations that they harness on a regular basis. Music, books, literature, cinema, philosophy, friends or family all point to what it will take to motivate the person in question.

Imagine how a teacher can use this to his or her advantage. Imagine how a manager or retailer could alter production if ambient motivation were monitored and/or made available. Imagine how you and your children will spend this weekend!

# PRACTICAL  CHALLENGE!

People tell me that they don't have time to harness ambient motivation. Forgive my first reaction. Here is a practical challenge to open up discovery and reading time in your life. Read only one page of the newspaper each day (your choice). Use the time that normally is spent on browsing through additional pages to grab a book or insightful source of ambient motivation and harness!

You can make a habit of reading motivational literature just as easily as you made a habit of reading doom and gloom in the evening paper!

Give this challenge one month of your time and then measure the results.

# A GOOD EXCUSE!

There is nothing quite as comfortable or forgiving as a good excuse. I have fallen into the waiting arms of a good excuse many times only to find out that it is a trap! Don' let a good excuse become your ambient motivation in life. Excuses are instant answers to "why" that provide little or no growth. Give up on excuses and promote motivation in your life, instead. You will find great rewards in this decision.

# UNFORGETTABLE!

I wondered how to end this project; whether to use a story or a powerful quotation or a reference from one of my ambient motivations? Following this next insert, you will find a resource list that provides you with a beginning to the journey down your action path.

But, I wanted something powerful and unforgettable in this section. I wanted something that would make a difference for both of us. I wanted a real situation or event that would sum up everything that I have been writing about! I thought back to so many object lessons over the years. I reviewed countless occasions during which I witnessed the power of harnessed ambient motivation. The list was mind-boggling!

On Sunday, November 24 my reality arrived! I can think of no greater example with which to reinforce the power of harnessed ambient motivation than the event that I am about to describe. I still find it difficult to believe that I was fortunate enough to be a witness. Sit back and enjoy and believe!

First, some background: One of my regular assignments is associated with teaching continuing education for educators in the Kansas City metro area. I research and develop courses that use a motivational approach to address acquisition of information that will benefit participants (each with a Master's degree) in the classroom. My recent assignment was to teach a two and one-half day workshop on popular and current literature with application to personal growth in the lives of teachers.

Needless to say, this is a major assignment that is both administrative and motivational in nature. It demands everything I have to give, and by the time the end of the course rolls around, everyone is absolutely exhausted and ready for a weekend off. But, since the course begins on Friday afternoon and ends on Sunday evening there is no weekend!

By Sunday afternoon, the participants are dragging their attention spans and inherent motivations from one speaker to another in hopes that Scotty will beam them up and away from the site, never to return.

My job is to excite the inherent motivation within each participant. My hope is that each will learn and enjoy what I, and my guest speakers, have to offer. Also, I make every effort to stretch the average attention span beyond its normal limits and keep things moving along as smoothly as possible.

On Friday evening, the energy level in the room is low. These educators have completed a full week of teaching with no time to themselves and a collective blood sugar level that would put most normal people in a coma.

By Sunday afternoon, everyone is focused on getting home to chores that are sorely neglected and a family that has accumulated a weekend-long list of complaints and conflicts. Included in the post-workshop package of knots to untie is the reality that a full teaching day will arrive in fifteen hours.

When I look up at 2:00 p.m., I see lots of yawning and slouching and frowning and I wonder if we will make it through the next two hours. With this in mind, try to imagine that you are the final speaker to address this group of 211 participants and that you will arrive at 2:30 p.m. to share humorous literature and entertaining insights into the world of laughter and its motivational prowess.

Such was the assignment delivered to David Naster, veteran comic and radio personality and current author of a soon-to-be-released book entitled, *"Sometimes you just have to laugh!"* Personally, I was worried that David's ability and insights would be wasted on this occasion. I was wrong!

During the 2:20 p.m. break David tapped me on the shoulder and smiled a big hello that radiated both motivation and enthusiasm. Looking at him, I felt as though a life preserver had been tossed to me in the middle of an unfriendly sea. We talked for a moment and then I prepared the audience for his presentation which was to include half a dozen humorous books and a one-on-one with David and his philosophy of humor in our lives. After I handed David the microphone I moved to an out-of-the-way spot and watched the crowd.

What I saw, astounded me. As a motivator with twenty-five years experience I have witnessed many "euphoric" presentations that lifted people up and presented them with renewed feelings of hope. I have heard "my-way" presentations that outlined options for success for hard workers and "multi-step" presentations that opened numerous doorways for highly dedicated self-starters.

*"But, I have never witnessed an event that matches what I witnessed in that room!"*

David unleashed ambient motivation , products, and professional prowess in a tour de force that filled the room with laughter and healed the woes of every one within sight and sound of his voice. People were laughing so hard and so honestly that it was difficult for them to stay seated. I laughed until the tears drenched my cheeks and I found myself immersed in an untapped source of ambient motivation.

By using books from the bookstore (ambient motivation) to detail his presentation on the power of humor (harnessing ambient motivation) David applied "my-step" and "multi-step" parameters to the event. By using his natural sense of humor and vast catalog of experiences to teach, David created a "euphoric" and healing reality for all of us.

Everybody laughed. Everybody cried. Everybody learned. Everybody received ambient motivation. As a result, everybody was better off. It was amazing! David did everything that I recommend for you and me and he did it with a flair of brilliance that few have mastered.

Believe this: Because of what David had done, the participants walked out with more motivation on Sunday afternoon than when they entered on Friday night. They drafted his ambient motivation and excited their own dwindling inherent motivation with its energy. They went back to the world with products and processes that would help them achieve what they want and need. And, I watched it happen! Amazing! One of the participants later told me that she had put his suggestions to work in the classroom on Monday morning!

Clearly, when David Naster walked into the room to present his talk on the healing power of humor, he had predicted, promoted, and protected his level of motivation with a high degree of success. He was the most motivated person in the entire room. He was flawless in his approach and he held the audience captive for one complete hour.

More amazing than anything I have stated thus far, David had no idea what he was going to find when he entered the room. The odds of failure are increased when effort is to be applied in unfamiliar territory. Imagine the effect of harnessing ambient motivation on the same level as I have described with full knowledge of what is waiting for you upon arrival at your destination!

The truth is, there is no limit to what you can accomplish in a similar frame of mind when you are concentrating on familiar surroundings.

I had the opportunity to watch everything that I believe in, and now stake my future upon, materialize right before my eyes. David was the embodiment of the ideas and activities that are the content of this book. Can you imagine how I felt?

## "Harnessing ambient motivation works!"

# MY CURRENT LIST OF AMBIENT MOTIVATION!

I would like to share some of my **current** favorites in the world of ambient motivation. But first, I thank you for reading this book. I hope that you have gained something in the process. I also hope to have the chance to include you in my seminar in the future.

*Note: I listed these according to my triangle of focus. But, I do not want to influence your perception of each product and its application to your focus.*

*Remember: This is a personal choice! We begin with audio tapes!*

First Things First
Stephen R. Covey
Simon & Schuster Audio
(Professional Focus)

Super Self
Charles J. Givens
Simon & Schuster
(Professional Focus)

Speak for Yourself
Robert Montgomery
Learn Incorporated
(Professional Focus)

Psycho-Cybernetics
Dr. Maxwell Maltz
Audio Renaissance Tapes
(Professional Focus)

The Leader In You
Dale Carnegie & Assoc.
Simon & Schuster Audio
(Professional Focus)

Stephanie Winston's Best
Organizing Tips
Simon & Schuster Audio
(Professional Focus)

52 Minutes To Turning
Your Life Around
David Viscott, M.D.
Audio Renaissance Tapes
(Professional Focus)

An Evening With George Burns
Dove Audio
(Personal Focus)

# BOOKS

first you have to row a little boat
Richard Bode
Warner Books
(? Focus)

20 Teachable Virtues
Barbara C. Unell
Jerry L. Wycoff Ph.D.
A Perigee Book
(Personal Focus)

Teaching Your Children Values
Linda and Richard Eyre
Simon & Schuster
(Personal Focus)

My Middle-Aged Baby Book
Mary-Lou Weisman
Workman Publishing
(Personal Focus)

Falling-Up
Shel Silverstein
HarperCollins
(Personal Focus)

When I Am an Old Woman
I Shall Wear Purple
Sandra Handelman Martz, Editor
Papier-Mache Press
(? Focus)

I Want To Grow Hair,
I Want To Grow Up,
I Want to Go to Boise
Erma Bombeck
Harper
(? Focus)

In Search of Excellence
Thomas J. Peters
Robert H. Waterman
Warner Books
(Professional Focus)

Days of Grace: A Memoir
Arthur Ashe
Arnold Rampersad
(? Focus)

Positive Discipline
Jane Nelsen, Ed.D.
Ballentine Books
(Personal Focus)

And If You Play Golf You're My Friend
Harvey Penick
Bud Shrake
Simon & Schuster
(? Focus)

The Hazards of Being Male
Herb Goldberg, Ph.D.
A Signet Book
(? Focus)

A 3rd Serving of
Chicken Soup for the Soul
Jack Canfield
Mark Victor Hansen
Health Communications
(? Focus)

From Beginning To End
Robert Fulghum
Ivy Books
(? Focus)

Having Our Say
Sarah L. Delany and Elizabeth Delany
Amy Hill Hearth
Dell Publishing
(? Focus)

They Call Me Coach
John Wooden
Jack Tobin
Contemporary Books
(Professional Focus)

Every Living Thing
James Herriot
St. Martin's
(Personal Focus)

The Seven Spiritual Laws of Success
Deepak Chopra
Amber-Allen
(? Focus)

Awaken The Giant Within
Anthony Robbins
Simon & Schuster
(Professional Focus)

Live Your Dreams
Les Brown
Morrow
(Professional Focus)

Wellness: Small Changes
You Can Use To
Make a Big Difference
Regina Sara Ryan and
John W. Travis, M.D.
Ten Speed Press
(Personal Focus)

# VIDEO TAPES

Rudy
Tri-Star
(? Focus)

The 50th Barbara Walters Special
MPI Home Video
(Professional Focus)

The Man Without A Face
Warner Home Video
(Personal Focus)

City Slickers
New Line Home Video
(Personal Focus)

The Black Stallion
MGM/UA Home Video
(Personal Focus)

Renaissance Man
Touchstone Home Video
(Professional Focus)

Ghost
Paramount Home Video
(? Focus)

Gung Ho
Paramount Home Video
(Professional Focus)

Grand Canyon
Fox Video
(? Focus)

Chariots of Fire
Warner Home Video
(? Focus)

Driving Miss Daisy
Warner Home Video
(Personal Focus)

The Paper
MCA Universal Home Video
(Professional Focus)

The Goonies
Warner Home Video
(Personal Focus)

Meatballs
HBO Video
(Professional Focus)

Rain Man
MGM/UA Home Video
(Personal Focus)

Hoosiers
Hemdale Film Corp.
(Professional Focus)

Apollo 13
MGM/UA Home Video
(Professional Focus)

Always
MCA Universal Home Video
(? Focus)

Starman
Columbia Tristar
(? Focus)

Field of Dreams
MCA Home Video
(Personal Focus)

# "For the serious and self-motivated who want to delve into the world of motivation at greater depth, I suggest the following!"

Title
*101 Recognition Secrets:*
*Tools for Motivating and Recognizing Today's Workforce*

Author
Rosalind Jefferies

ISBN
0-9648444-2-7

---

Title
*The Achievement Zone: Eight Skills for Winning All the Time*
*from the Playing Field to the Boardroom*

Author
Shane Murphy

ISBN
0-399-14096-4

---

Title
*Handbook of Motivation and Cognition,*
*Vol.3: The Interpersonal*
*Context*

Author
Edited by Richard M. Sorrentino and E. Tony Higgins

ISBN
1-57230-052-3

Title
*Motivating Quotes for Motivated People*

Author
Susanne Stark.
Edited by Patrick Caton

ISBN
1-56245-241-X

Title
*Motivation and Leadership at Work*

Author
Richard Steers, Lyman Porter and Gregory Bigley

ISBN
0-07-061031-2

Title
*Motivation: Theory, Research and Application*

Author
Herbert L. Petri

ISBN
0-534-20460-0

Title
*The Psychology of a Resume That Stands Out:*
*Common Sense Principles to Help You Think,*
*Act and Live More Abundantly*

Author
Travis Young

ISBN
0-9650566-1-9

Title
*RX for Business:*
*A Troubleshooting Guide for*
*Building a High-Performance Organization.*

Author
Mark G. Brown, Darcy E. Hitchcock
and Marsha L. Willard

ISBN
0-614-12582-0

---

Title
*The Seven Levels of Change:*
*The Secrets Used by the World's Largest Corporations*
*to Create, Innovate, and Motivate.*

Author
Rolf Smith

ISBN
1-56530-207-9

---

Title
*Success Secrets of the Motivational Superstars:*
*America's Greatest Speakers Reveal Their Secrets*

Author
Michael Jeffreys

ISBN
0-7615-0612-8

Title
*Why We Do What We Do:*
*Understanding Self-Motivation*

Author
Edward Deci and Richard Flaste

ISBN
0-14-025526-5

---

Title
*150 Ways to Increase Intrinsic Motivation*
*in the Classroom*

Author
James P. Raffini

ISBN
0-205-16567-2

---

Title
*Coaching in the Classroom:*
*Teaching Self-Motivation*

Author
Grant Teaff

ISBN
1-55502-703-2

Title
*Emotion and Motivation*

Author
Edited by Brian Parkinson and
Andrew M. Colman

ISBN
0-582-27808-2

---

Title
*Empowering Employees*

Author
L. Kristi Long

ISBN
0-7863-0314-X

---

Title
*Fabled Service: Ordinary Acts,
Extraordinary Outcomes*

Author
Elizabeth A. Sanders

ISBN
0-89384-270-2

Title
*Finding a Way to Win:*
*The Principles of Leadership,*
*Teamwork and Motivation*

Author
Bill Parcels

ISBN
0-385-48122-5

---

Title
*Get Everyone in Your*
*Boat Rowing in the Same Direction:*
*5 Leadership Principles to*
*Follow So Others Will Follow You*

Author
Bob Boylan

ISBN
1-55850-547-4

---

Title
*Leading at Mach 2*

Author
Steve Sullivan

ISBN
0-9641053-1-4

Title
*The Little Book of Big Motivation:*
*One Hundred Eighty Simple Ways to*
*Overcome Obstacles and Realize Your Goals*

Author
Eric Jensen

ISBN
0-449-90946-8

---

Title
*Managing Generation X:*
*How to Bring Out the Best in Young Talent*

Author
Bruce Tulgin

ISBN
1-56343-111-4

---

Title
*The Motivating Team Leader*

Author
Lewis E. Losoncy

ISBN
1-884015-82-4

Title
*Nebraska Symposium on Motivation, 1994:*
*The Individual, the Family, and Social Good:*
*Personal Fulfillment in Times of Change*

Author
Edited by Gary B. Melton

ISBN
0-8032-8221-4

Title
*Paulson on Change*

Author
Terry Paulson

ISBN
1-882180-49-6

Title
*Psychology for Leaders:*
*Using Motivation, Conflict, and*
*Power to Manage More Effectively.*

Author
Dean Tjosvold

ISBN
0-471-59755-4

Title
*Raising Achievers:*
*A Parent's Plan for Motivating Children to Excel*

Author
Nita Weis

ISBN
0-8054-6160-4

---

Title
*Resiliency: How to Bounce Back*
*Faster, Stronger, Smarter!*

Author
Tessa A. Warschaw and Dee Barlow

ISBN
1-57101-021-1

---

Title
*Rewarding and Recognizing Employees:*
*Ideas for Individuals, Teams and Managers*

Author
Joan P. Klubnik

ISBN
0-7863-0297-6

Title
*The Simple Art of Greatness:*
*Building, Managing, and*
*Motivating a Kick-Ass WorkForce*

Author
James X. Mullen

ISBN
0-670-85211-2

Title
*Student Motivation*

Author
Paul R. Pintrich and
Dale H. Schunk

ISBN
0-02-395621-6

Title
*Super-Motivation: A Blueprint for*
*Energizing Your Organization from Top to Bottom*

Author
Dean R. Spitzer

ISBN
0-8144-0286-0

Title
*Why Work?: Motivating the New Workforce*

Author
Michael Macoby

ISBN
0-917917-05-7

Title
*The Corporate Coach: How to Build a Team of Loyal Customers and Happy Employees*

Author
James B. Miller, Paul B. Brown

ISBN
0-88730-685-3

Title
*Doing and Rewarding:*
*Inside a High-Performance Organization*

Author
Carl G. Thor

ISBN
1-56327-061-7

Title
*Get Motivated!: Daily Psyche-Ups*

Author
Kara Leverte Farley and Sheila M. Curry

ISBN
0-671-88100-0

Title
*Group Motivation: Social Psychological Perspectives*

Author
Michael Hogg and Dominic Abrams

ISBN
0-13-302126-2

Title
*How to Recognize and Reward Employees*

Author
Donna Deeprose

ISBN
0-8144-7832-8

Title
*Management Plus: Leadership,*
*Motivation and Power in the Changing Marketplace*

Author
Lloyd Smigel

ISBN
1-56565-159-6

Title

*Management Plus:  Managing Productivity Through Motivation, Performance, and Commitment*

Author
Robert A. Fazzi

ISBN
1-55623-756-1

Title

*Meditations  For Surviving Without Cigarettes*

Author
Esther Wanning

ISBN
0-380-76916-6

Title
*Miracle of Motivation*

Author
George Shinn

ISBN
0-8423-3967-1

Title
*Motivating Superior Performance*

Author
Saul W. Gellerman

ISBN
1-56327-063-3

---

Title
*One Hundred Ways to Enhance Self-Concept
in the Classroom*

Author
Jack Caufield and Harold C. Wells

ISBN
0-205-15415-8

---

Title
*Reaching the Peak Performance Zone:
How to Motivate Yourself and Others to Excel*

Author
Gerald Kushel

ISBN
0-8144-0222-4

Title
*Selling at Mach 1: Motivational Acceleration*

Author
Steven D. Sullivan

ISBN
0-9641053-0-6

---

Title
*Straight Up!: A Teenager's Guide to
Taking Charge of Your Life*

Author
Elizabeth Taylor-Gerdes

ISBN
1-885242-00-X

---

Title
*Thresholds of Motivation:
Nurturing Human Growth in the Organization*

Author
V. S. Mahesh

ISBN
0-07-462232-3

Title
*Values-Based Leadership:*
*Rebuilding Employee Commitment,*
*Performance and Productivity*

Author
Thomas D. Kuczmarski

ISBN
0-13-121856-5

Title
*Daily Motivations for African-American Success*

Author
Dennis Kimbro

ISBN
0-449-90786-4

Title
*Don't Quit: Motivation and*
*Exercises to Bring Out the Winner in You*

Author
Jake Steinfeld

ISBN
0-446-39485-8

Title
*Motivating at Work*

Author
Twyla Dell

ISBN
1-56052-201-1

Title
*Motivation and Goal Setting*

Author
Edited by Career Press Staff

ISBN
1-56414-111-X

Title
*Motivation at Work*

Author
Jane R. Miskell and Vincent Miskell

ISBN
1-55623-868-1

Title
*Motivation in The Real World*

Author
Saul Gellerman

ISBN
0-453-00831-3

Title
*Patterns of High Performance:*
*Discovering the Ways People Work Best*

Author
Jerry L. Fletcher

ISBN
1-881052-70-2

Title
*Positive Thinking Everyday:*
*An Inspiration for Each Day of the Year.*

Author
Norman Vincent Peale

ISBN
0-671-86891-8

Title
*Psychology of Motivation*
*(2 Cassettes)*

Author
Denis Waitley

ISBN
0-671-79640-2

Title
*They Can But They Don't:*
*Helping Students Overcome Work Inhibition*

Author
Jerome H. Bruns

ISBN
0-14-015229-6

---

Title
*Thoroughly Fit:*
*How to Make a Lifestyle Change in 90 Days:*
*A Motivational Devotional Journal*

Author
Becky Tirabassi and Candice Copeland-Brooks

ISBN
0-310-40301-4

---

Title
*Winning Commitment:*
*How to Build and Keep a Competitive Workforce*

Author
Gary Dressler

ISBN
0-07-016630-7

Title
*Change Your Mind, Change Your World*

Author
Richard Gillett

ISBN
0-671-73538-1

---

Title
*Football Coach's Survival Guide*

Author
Michael D. Koehler

ISBN
0-13-324187-4

---

Title
*Human Motives and Cultural Models*

Author
Edited by Roy G. D'Andrade and Claudia Strauss

ISBN
0-521-42338-4

---

Title
*Open and Utility Training: The Motivational Method*

Author
Jack Volhard and Wendy Volhard

ISBN
0-87605-755-5

Title
*Soar With Your Strengths*

Author
Donald O. Clifton

ISBN
0-385-30414-5

Title
*Coaching and Motivation*

Author
William E. Warren

ISBN
0-13-140203-X

Title
*Motivating People*

Author
Dayle M. Smith

ISBN
0-8120-4673-0

Title
*Motivation*

Author
Harvard Business Review Staff

ISBN
0-87584-263-1

Title
*Motivation and Work Behavior*

Author
Richard M. Steers

ISBN
0-07—060956-X

Title
*Teach Yourself to Win*

Author
Steve Stone

ISBN
0-929387-54-6

Title
*Understanding Action: An Essay on Reasons*

Author
Frederic Schick

ISBN
0-521-40886-5

Title
*Communicate for Success:*
*How to Manage, Motivate and Lead Your People*

Author
Eric W. Skopec

ISBN
0-201-10528-4

Title
*Explaining Human Action*

Author
Kathleen Lennon

ISBN
0-8126-9135-0

---

Title
*Maslow's Motivation and Personality*

Author
Robert Frager and James Fadiman

ISBN
0-06-041987-3

---

Title
*Human Motivation*

Author
David C. McClelland

ISBN
0-521-36951-7

---

Title
*Born to Win*

Author
Lewis Timberlake and Marietta Reed

ISBN
0-8423-0338-3

Title
*Motivation: The Organization of*
*Animal and Human Action*

Author
Douglas Mook

ISBN
0-393-95474-9

---

Title
*The Manager's Motivation Desk Book*

Author
Thomas L. Quick

ISBN
0-471-88377-8

---

Title
*Sales Cybernetics: New Scientific*
*Techniques in Motivational Selling*

Author
Brian Adams

ISBN
0-87980-412-2

Title
*Peak Performance Principles for High Achievers*

Author
John R. Noe

ISBN
0-8119-0648-5

---

Title
*Coaching and Motivation: A
Practical Guide to Maximum Athletic Performance*

Author
William E. Warren

ISBN
0-13-138990-4

---

Title
*Now Is Your Time to Win*

Author
Dave Dean

ISBN
0-8423-4727-5

---

Title
*Be a Motivational Leader*

Author
Leroy Eims

ISBN
0-89693-008-4

Title
*A Rhetoric of Motives*

Author
Kenneth Burke

ISBN
0-520-01546-0

Title
*Toward a Psychology of Being*

Author
Abraham H. Maslow

ISBN
0-442-03805-4

Title
*2 Minute Motivation:  How to*
*Inspire Superior Performance*

Author
Robert W. Wendover

ISBN
1-57071-019-8

Title
*Eager to Learn: Helping Children
Become Motivated and Love Learning*

Author
Raymond J. Wlodkowski and Judith H. Jaynes

ISBN
1-55542-206-3

---

Title
*Get It Done: A Guide to
Motivation, Determination and Achievement*

Author
Ian McMahan

ISBN
0-3807-7970-6

ONCE AGAIN, I thank you for reading this book. If you wish to bring the "Harnessing Motivation" seminar to your location, send your inquiry to:

Educational Management
P.O. Box 3478
Olathe, Kansas 66063-3478

or e-mail
EducationalManagement@worldnet.att.net